Gateway to the V

of the Spirit World

Christine

Table of Content

Dedication

I would like to dedicate this book to my family, Charlotte, James, Jacqueline and Melanie-Morgan. Also to the patience and understanding of my husband Robert who has endeavoured to encourage me over the years.

Acknowledgements

I wish to express my special thanks of gratitude to my husband, Robert, who has always supported and encouraged my development. To my eldest daughter Charlotte, who accepted the unexplained corridors and vortexes of ice-cold hurricane type wind, which occurred even though there were no windows or doors open. She would simply open her bedroom door and window allowing the icy breeze to flow out into the garden. To my only son James, who too experienced much phenomena. How I enjoyed our exchange of experiences. To my second eldest daughter Jacqueline and youngest daughter Melanie-Morgan who also experienced unexplained activity whilst at home with me and I am sure, would whole-heartedly agree that there is so much unexplained science to be researched.

To my late mom and dad, who were also part of my development. My mother, Muriel, who was a non-practising medium, and my father, George, who was a trance medium. How I enjoyed our conversations about the very strange, scary, bewildering phenomena he too experienced; also for his continued presence in my life with conversations and messages through mediumship.

My friend and colleague Chris Billington and all the laughter and fun we had with our psychic/mediumship shows in Australia. I will never forget when we sat together in our circle of three and the physical phenomena we experienced.

To all the truly professional teachers and mentors whom I have had the privilege and honour to have worked with.

To my mentor Matthew Smith I give thanks for the hours of one-to-one mentorship and the many weeks of tutoring. Your encouragement, patience and professionalism provided me with a firm platform for my mental mediumship. My thanks to Eileen Davies, who encouraged calmness and listening skills with spirit in the most natural, normal way and to listen only to the spirit and avoid distractions when giving a reading.

My gratitude to Scott Milligan, physical medium, to whom I give tremendous respect. Thank you for mentoring me for 12 months, generously nurturing my personal spiritual connection through your own development and spiritual powers. Thank you also for your weekend courses and your strength and ability to go public, bringing teachings to the world. Your teachings and your sharing have been a great strength to me, and I am sure the unseen world must love you for all the work you do. I wish to acknowledge David Thompson, physical medium, for the privilege of participating in your physical mediumship demonstrations.

You have such an amazingly spiritual connection, and I am honoured to have crossed your path on my journey. I give love and gratitude to the late Glen Edwards for the encouragement and strength to continue my exploration with mediumship. I wish to also acknowledge Rick Collingwood, teacher and mentor of hypnosis with whom, over the years of training, opened my mind to the power of the subconscious mind and its limitless capabilities.

I wish to acknowledge my first tutor, Rose Owen. Thank you, Rose, for all those weeks of professional practice you allowed me to participate in as well as your weekend retreats. You were always professional and provided me with a firm platform from which to really start to work. Thank you for recommending my mediumship ability to the Rainbow Girls, who ran a spiritual church where I indulged my mental mediumship.

I also wish to acknowledge Nick and Steve at the Banyan Retreat for providing the platform to learn and develop my mediumship through top professional mediums. Your services honoured all who were developing, and without you, the work of the spirit would not have been possible. I live in gratitude for your work.

I also wish to acknowledge John Hart and his team at Amazon Publishing Pro, as without the guidance and advice of your service, my book may never have been published.

I give love and gratitude to all the people in my life who have helped form who I have become.

Most of all, I acknowledge and give love and respect to my spirit team, who have always inspired, trained and guided me. I promise I will do all I can to open the eyes and hearts of people, so they know they are never alone, that they are loved and are so much more than who they think they are. That they, too, can change their outlook and know just how truly powerful they really are.

On behalf of myself and my spirit team, we wish you all the power and sensitivity of the spirit within your life.

Through Mediumship We Touch.

Christine

About the Author

Christine has been a successful practising hypnotherapist, kinesiologist, healer, and psychic medium for over twenty years in the United Kingdom and Western Australia. Spirit communication began for her whilst in the United Kingdom and increased exponentially whilst in the Northern Territory and then in Western Australia. Mediumship and telepathy had become a regular daily experience as information was being received from her spirit friends about family members, their circumstances, as well as general concerns and interesting future events.

Through the encouragement of her spirit friends, Christine has continuously trained her abilities and has been mentored by some of the top mediums in the United Kingdom and Australia. More recently, Christine has held many spiritual mediumistic reading events, worked on a church platform, held one-to-one personal and telephone readings, and administered Reiki healing, clinical hypnosis, and Kinesiology sessions.

Christine is passionate about the need to share and open up awareness for individuals in order that everyone has the opportunity to recognise their own abilities and look towards the Gateway to the Wonders of the Spirit World.

Section One: Through Mediumship We Touch

Gateway to the Wonders of the Spirit World

Through Mediumship We Touch

Even as a young girl, during the summer holidays, I would always try to encourage my friends to sit with me in a circle to see if there were any garden spirits around. I always discovered I was on my own with this. So I would sit on my swing and sing until I reached a point of semi-trance. I was very aware of the energy and personality of people and friends around me and was very street-wise.

My first real conscious knowing came to me when I was at College doing a Secretarial Course. I wasn't really interested in being a secretary, but in those days, it was expected of young women to become a secretary. They said it was always a skill you could fall back on. I remember looking at my tutor, who was writing on the chalkboard. As she looked at me, I knew without a doubt that I, too, would be a lecturer, except that I would have more responsibility. Then the moment passed, and I merely continued with my studies. Less than five years later, this came to pass. I obtained a full-time lectureship with several colleges of further and higher education over a span of twenty-five years. I held positions of Programme Manager, Curriculum Developer, and Careers Officer alongside the full-time lecturing positions.

I have been aware of many sign posts in my life which have taken me in different directions. I have received messages in my dreams which were self-prophetic, travelled half way around the world, had four beautiful children who now have their own families, and returned to the United Kingdom as if I have come full circle, waiting for the next phase.

Over the last thirty-plus years, I have developed and continually trained my mediumistic abilities being able to read mediumistically and psychically as well as provide healing energy through Reiki. I am a practising medium and have been for decades, but as time continues, my skills and abilities have extended and deepened.

I decided to write a short book on my mediumistic experiences to aid you, the reader, in exploring your own mediumistic awareness from the point of view of joy and happiness. To be inspired to listen and become aware of the energy around you and to remind your soul, your spirit, that you are never alone. There is always love around you. The power of prayer has no limits.

Mediumship is a wonderful craft as it is through mediumship that we 'touch.' We touch heavenly power and love, we can become inspired and motivated to connect to healing energy. Through mediumship, it is possible to connect with other dimensions, knowledge beyond our knowing, the godly spheres, spiritual spheres, and much

3

more. Mediumship is just the tip of the iceberg, and I am sure in years to come, much more work will be conducted through genuine mediumship abilities.

Many people have proudly admitted they have experienced déjà vu. It's the experience of feeling you have been in this situation before. Some people can also provide accurate detail of buildings and rooms, including decor. Many people now feel able to express their near-death experiences of a heavenly place that is beautiful and loving. Many recount that they were returned so they could carry out a mission or follow through with instructions for specific work.

The ability to 'touch through the power of mediumship' opens many doorways into the spiritual realms, as mediums are able to connect with loved ones, not only for themselves but for others too. Contact can provide comfort, closure, and knowledge that loved ones still reside, but on a different vibrational frequency, and that it is only our physical body that returns to the earth. The power of true connection is love from our dimension to another and vice versa.

A true medium has the accomplished ability to connect with a power that facilitates vision and awareness of the past, present and future environments beyond our five senses and physical ability. My dearest mother, who began to lose her hearing in her later years when turning into the great power of mediumistic ability, suddenly experienced perfect hearing. My dear father also tapped into mediumistic power as he would suddenly receive information on how to solve a mechanical problem that he had not previously thought of and, in fact, initiated several inventions from adaptations of engines. The list continues, but only recently have people begun to question the source of this power we can tap into, which can awaken and extend our existing ability.

Mediumship is a science. A new science that would surely compel leading scientists to investigate in an ethical and respectful manner a medium whereby the medium is not used as a rat lab or purely as a tool for those who would wish to gain personal notoriety without personal experience.

My journey with mediumship has been long and hard. I have discovered that there is always another depth to reach. Just when I think I have experienced everything, I realise I am still at the tip of the iceberg, and there is so much more to experience and understand. I have trained my abilities for over 22 years. I am also accomplished in the healing art of Reiki, Kinesiology, and Clinical Hypnosis.

This book is my truth and all the stories contained are true experiences of mediumistic attunement in action. I hold all my experiences sacred even though, at the time, I was often scared. There is nothing I would change. I will continue delving deeper into the different vibrational realms and dimensions to the best of my ability in order to hopefully awaken those who would enjoy exploring the ability of their mind and to be open to all the wonderful experiences through mediumship.

I hope you enjoy the stories as well as touching that part of you that would like to explore this truth for yourself in your own way in order to know and understand how wonderful you really are.

I wish you happy reading and hope you enjoy a sample of some true experiences of a medium.

Enjoy

Christine

Author

Jacqueline – Ghostly Apparition

The Northern Territory in Australia is a beautiful place. I remember getting off the Ghan train in Alice Springs (the Ghan is a train service that operates from east to west Australia taking a southern route) to be welcomed by the hot air, scorched land, and landscape covered the most beautiful shades of red, orange, and yellow. There were mountainous hills covered in bush in the distance and a sense of an outback cowboy and Indian country as I used to see on tv. As soon as I stepped onto the land, I felt this overwhelming feeling of peace and tranquillity. At that moment, I decided this would be where we would live for a while. The people were friendly and helpful, and after the many long winters in the UK, I felt that I was at last beginning to thaw.

While waiting for our belongings to arrive by the next train, we stayed at a local motel and began searching for a rental property immediately. We were lucky as there were quite a few rentals available, and within a few days, we were settled with our belongings in a lovely bungalow opposite a park. We made some wonderful friends in Alice Springs, and the children thrived. Alice Springs is a spiritual town with several spiritual churches. I realised quite soon that the church was the main entertainment area, with a musical band playing at every session.

They organised spiritual speakers from all over Australia to talk about spiritual matters. One guest speaker held a couple of sessions so we could experience how powerful the mind was when connected to universal energy. We actually experienced particles of gold in our hands, and some people who had fillings turned them into gold. It was an amazing experience, and the spiritual church was doing a wonderful job.

***

It was now the weekend and we decided to take a bit of a rest from the week's activities. That evening my daughter Jacqueline, came up to me for a cuddle as we all watched tv. We sat together as we watched a film until bedtime. Soon the children were in bed. It had been a hot day, and as the evening came around, a cool breeze blew through the opened windows. Very soon, we had all gone to bed.

It was the middle of the night when I woke up for some reason.

The room was very dark, almost pitch black, and I could not see anything. I was wondering why I had woken up. Perhaps one of the children had come into the bedroom, or had the family dog needed to go outside, I wasn't sure. I sat up in bed to listen carefully around the house. As I listened, my side of the bed immediately caught my attention, and I began to feel that one of the children had entered the bedroom and was standing near me. I glared into the darkness of the room. There was no sound to be heard. In my mind, I was thinking, "I can see you. I know you are there."

As I was thinking these words, I could feel myself smiling. Suddenly and amazingly, through the darkness, I began to see the outline of my daughter Jacqueline. The more I gazed and concentrated, the clearer her image became. I also noticed that she was wearing the spice girl tee shirt she had been wearing in the lounge the night before. Then I saw her face and her hair. The skin on her face was perfect, it slightly glistened and seemed rather illuminated and her hair was perfect, beautifully brushed with her dark brown hair shining as I had never seen before. She stood outside my arms range and seemed to move towards the end of the bed and turn as if she was responding to someone. I immediately thought, oh okay, so your sisters and brother are here too. As she turned again to face me, I reached out, saying, "Come on then," to pull her into my bed.

As I did so, my hand went straight through the apparition of my daughter. I was shocked. The apparition knew I was shocked and quickly disappeared. Suddenly there was nobody there, and the room was again in total darkness!

The following morning I immediately went into Jacqueline's bedroom to find her already up. I compared the real image of my daughter to the apparition I saw of her the previous night.

The apparition of my daughter was produced in perfection. My reality of my daughter was that of an active, happy girl with unkempt hair and skin that did not illuminate.

I can only assume that the spirit world wanted me to see them. They took the form of someone I loved dearly, so I would accept them. I did not see who was at the bottom of my bed. Nor do I know why they chose Jacqueline, perhaps because I was cuddling her hours before the apparition.

Some days, I would find myself asking the same question repeatedly, which was when people say they see their loved ones whether it is, in fact, their loved one as certainly the apparition I saw was my daughter who was alive and well.

Is it so easy for the spirit world to impersonate someone? I was never afraid of what I saw; it just posed many questions to me. But most certainly, there is a phenomena, a power that is real. There may be many theories about what I experienced that night.

I like to think that the spirit world came to me and wanted me to know they were around me, didn't want to frighten me, and so took the apparition of my daughter. Maybe you have your own theory?

A Night to Remember

I had just moved to Perth, Western Australia, with my four children. We would receive a free weekly newspaper that gave local news and local adverts for traders, services, and local events. I used to occasionally flick through the paper until, one day, I felt the need to look at every advertisement. I didn't know why or what I was looking for, except that I knew something was going to interest me. Then one week, when I was in the kitchen skimming through the paper, I noticed an event advertised. It was entitled 'A Night to Remember' and organised by two psychic medium sisters. That sounds interesting, I thought, the tickets were very reasonable, and the venue was in the next town. I made contact and bought a ticket.

It was a wet, dirty night, and I had little idea how to locate the community hall where the venue was being held, but I was aware of the general direction. Arriving late, I was greeted in the car park by a lady who asked me if I was attending the event. She escorted me in when I realised I was the last member of the audience to arrive and they had been waiting for me.

The hall had been decorated with psychic art portraits painted under trance conditions by the two psychic sisters. The spirit world had wanted them to produce art to encourage and inspire future psychic artists. Some I liked, others I was not sure about, but there was plenty of colour, and they were designed beautifully. At the back of the hall, the psychic sisters had placed a couple of trestle tables where there were a couple of urns of hot water with tea, coffee, sugar, and plain biscuits available during the interval. The people in the hall seemed very nice.

Then the event began. Apparently, there were supposed to be three sisters, but one sister was unwell and had to stand down, so the two remaining worked a little harder. The two psychic sisters proceeded to give psychic/mediumship messages to members of the audience, which there must have been in the region of two hundred people. At some point during the course of the first half of the event, one of the sisters looked directly at me, stating that there was no coincidence where people were sitting in the hall. That the seat we were on had been arranged by spirit, even the people we were sitting next to. I checked along the line of people who were in the back row with me. They all knew each other well and were from the local church. The lady directly next to me smiled at me and asked if I was a Reiki healer. I had never heard of Reiki, and neither was I aware of the healing arts as I know of them now (Reiki is a Japanese healing modality). The lady then asked if I needed healing. I hesitantly replied, "yes," as I had suffered a lot of pain in my neck, particularly when I lay down. She asked if she could heal me during the interval, and I surprisingly said yes.

The interval soon came around, and members of the audience were making their way to the back of the hall, where tea and coffee were being served. The lady next to me asked if I was able to ignore all the people around me whilst she worked on healing me. I thought if I closed my eyes, I could. In any case, I didn't know anyone and certainly would not be seeing them again, so I complied with everything she asked of me.

As I continued to sit on the hard wooden chair, she stood up behind me and gently placed her hands on my shoulders. I kept my eyes shut to avoid any distractions. Within just a few seconds, I was aware of a choir singing, and then she began gently rocking me backwards and forwards. I felt great comfort being rocked so gently, listening to what seemed like a choir singing. I was then aware of incredible energy forming at the back of my neck, which gradually proceeded to move gently upwards into the back of my head and then downwards, gradually reaching under my shoulder blades. The very warm energy ultimately went up into the back of my head, then down around into my shoulder blades, and this continued for several minutes. It was so very relaxing; I felt that I was being taken to a different place in time and space. I thought I also heard my lady healer singing with the choir and wondered whether I should also hum along with her. Shortly after this wonderful, energetic experience, the warm energy I had experienced suddenly went cold. The gentle rocking stopped. The singing of the choir stopped. It seemed everything stopped, and then the lady removed her hands. All this was done in no longer than fifteen minutes, in fact, much less time. I asked her if she had been singing. She replied that no she had not been singing. It was through the healing connection that I had been privileged to hear the choir and singing. As I was taking in my wonderful experience, all I said to this wonderful healer was, "Thank you". Thank you did not seem anywhere near enough gratitude as I have never had any problems with my neck since. I am, however, very careful with my neck from now on with pillows.

As I had such a wonderful experience, I decided that I wanted to learn how to do this so I, too, could help people out of pain and into health.

Over time I learned Reiki and gained a lot of practise every day over decades with different people and their health. I later became a Reiki Master and Teacher and have attuned others to enable them to be Reiki practitioners. I also realised that although my wonderful healer lady said she practised Reiki, I now understand she was a healing medium who had the ability to directly connect with healers in the spirit world. My ability as a Reiki Master/Teacher was only the very beginning, and so my journey was about to begin.

It was at this point that I became hungry to learn more of this power, this energy that we could utilise and tap into to heal, and the many more things we could learn and do as human beings that I had never been aware of before. I knew there was so very much more to our lives than we were aware of. Yet somewhere, somehow, we had forgotten who we are, forgotten our capabilities, and maybe even forgotten why we are here in the physical and the meaning of our life.

We are so very much more than we have been led to understand. Have we been silenced over the centuries? Is our society so scared that should humanity realise our true potential and begin to use it, we would no longer be in slavery to egoism, controllers, or those who pretend they are doing their best for us?

Definitely worth a thought! But we must awaken first!

I believe that being attuned to the Universal Power either through Reiki attunements or prayer is a gateway to the wonders of the spirit world, with knowledge and abilities beyond our present understanding. Through my experience of being healed through energy and the very many hours of healing and attunements I have given, I can only say how much my life path has changed.

Personally, I would recommend Reiki and trance healing to anyone who is open to it.

Section Two: My Wonderful Spirit Communicator

A Gift of Love from my Wise Spirit Friend

Having moved to Western Australia, I had been planning to return to the United Kingdom the following summer to see my mother and was considering which dates would be the best. As the UK summertime was still quite a few months ahead, I looked online to see which courses were being held in London so I could incorporate a course or two whilst in the UK.

During this decision time, my spirit friend came to visit me during my dreams. I was taken to my old childhood bedroom, which was at the back of the house and overlooked a well-groomed and manicured garden. My wise spirit friend was always encouraging and inspirational. My deceased father greeted me and introduced me to another spirit friend who came over as very loving and caring.

My spirit messenger wanted to convey a message to me. He placed what looked like a poster on my wardrobe door, which looked like a cartoon comic magazine. It showed frame by frame my life journey from the moment I was born to the end of my life in the physical world pictorially. It did not seem to make much sense to me as I was unable to see the pictures clearly.

He drew my attention to a particular couple of window chapters from which he began explaining the story. Then my friend said, "you might get some flowers." I accepted the information and continued to look at the comic strip, which seemed to encompass everything that was going to happen in my life right to the end.

My friend then turned his head, and I suddenly noticed that the back of his hair was very wispy and grey, which gave away the fact that he was a very elderly man, different to his initial introduction, which would have been around the age of forty. I felt very comfortable with my friend and enjoyed his companionship. He felt wordily and knowledgeable and wanted to inspire me in my mediumship for the future. I was as excited as he was.

The dream faded, and I wrote down in my journal about my visit from my spirit friend.

The weeks and months passed, and I had put to the background the exciting information given to me. It did not mean anything to me at the time, and I forgot about it until my return to the UK. I had booked a trance mediumship course in London. Unknown to me, even when on the first couple of days of the course, there was a physical medium on the same course as myself. Furthermore, we were sitting at the same dinner table, and I loved to listen to his stories about his mediumship experiences. He came over as a wonderful person, full of integrity and very open and honest and happy to share what he knew. I was completely unaware that he had been sitting for physical mediumship or was himself a physical medium. It was a wonderful week, full of laughter and facilitated a deeper connection with the spirit world for me.

Then it became interesting, as a rumour was going around that he was going to hold a physical mediumship demonstration on the Tuesday and Thursday of that week.

Suddenly, my memory of my spirit friend came flooding back. Goodness, I thought I was going to get some flowers! It all instantly made sense of that visitation message, and now it was coming to fruition. The power of the spirit world and my wonderful friends had told me about this, but I just had to wait. They have never told me wrong, never, and I know whatever they tell me will always be right.

I became so very excited on a number of counts that I had been foretold of this event and that now it was happening. How did they know this would happen? How did they know I would be on this course? How did they know I would be sitting at the same dinner table as this physical medium? What did he experience? How did it feel? What happens?

Millions of questions I wanted to ask.

I was becoming rather sorry for him being bombarded with my excitable questions. Then I decided to tell him about my spirit friend and my visitation message. I began to notice that people were listening and so slightly changed the conversation by saying that "I had ordered some flowers" rather than I was told the spirit world were going to apport me some flowers. I felt that it sounded better amongst people at the table to phrase it this way.

The first group of sitters took place on Tuesday. My group sitting was on Thursday. The group I was in took lessons in the Sanctuary, which we all enjoyed.

My roommate was on Tuesday, and when she returned, she was so excited and wanted to tell me everything; however, they had been told not to say anything until after the Thursday group had experienced the phenomena.

Finally, Thursday came, and I was so excited. We were given a half-hour talk prior to confirming that everyone was happy to follow the rules.

The séance was about to begin, and as I sat with my back to the heavily curtained windows, I was are of the spirit world standing behind me and stroking the back left-hand side of my hair in a downward movement, reminding me that something special might take place for me that evening.

A whole range of physical mediumship took place that evening. I could smell and taste the unique aspect of ectoplasm which left its imprint on me even to this day. Even now, I can suddenly experience the taste and odour of ectoplasm which seems to waft through me and around me at odd times during the day and night.

As the séance continued, the spirit team connected to the physical medium greeted us and spoke to us at length, answering questions from the circle that evening.

Then, just as the spirit world informed me, a spirit team member declared that he wished to speak to a lady from Australia. A lady a few seats away from me said "yes," then I slowly said "yes" also.

The circle members laughed, and then he said, "I want to speak to the lady who ordered the flowers". I immediately said yes. Eric had found me! "I understand you have put an order in for some flowers? Why don't you go around the College and collect the flowers if that is what you want"? I didn't reply. I was so amazed at the phenomena I was not only spellbound but speechless! "You cannot take the flowers back with you.

Do you like Rhinos"? I felt like a two-year-old compared to the spirit guide and replied, "Do you mean a Rhinoceros"? He said, "Yes." "Are you going to apport a rhinoceros into the room?" Everyone in the room laughed at the thought of a rhino suddenly appearing in the middle of the room, most probably feeling rather confused. He paused for a while and then returned, stating that there was not enough energy to apport a rhino. "Do you like gold?" My heart dropped, and I began to think of my gold earrings upstairs in my room being apported, or even a piece of gold. The thought of gold did nothing for me. I was brought up in a family that worked with bullion. It is a dirty metal, and it smells awful in its raw state, nothing pleasant about it. I did not even consider it to have any worth, contradictory to society and, therefore, its price tag.

Eric must have picked up on my disappointment "yes." Then he said, "Actually, it's not gold, but a gold coloured. It comes from the Brecon Beacon. Do you know where this is?" I said, "yes."

The Brecon Beacon is in Wales and has been used by the military to train soldiers on navigation, map reading and outdoor survival. "It belonged to a boy who held nothing sacred". With that, he spoke to a circle member and asked that when she either heard something or felt something drop to tell him straight away. The circle member agreed, and the séance moved on. At regular intervals, the spirit guide would ask the circle member if anything had dropped near her and, on several occasions, answered no. The spirit communicator said that it took a lot of concentration and focus to apport something, and if the concentration was lost, the object would not appear.

After about twenty to thirty minutes, it was reported that something had dropped near her.

The spirit guide requested that she pick it up. My apport had manifested. How wonderful and privileged I was not only to be able to participate in a physical mediumship demonstration but also to be made to feel so special in the spirit world apporting something to me.

At the end of the séance, the object was being passed up the line of people who were examining it. Most people had left the room by now, and I still had not received it and had to ask where it was and if I could please have it. Finally, I received it. It was a coin. A gold-coloured World Saver for the Black Rhinoceros 1992. I remember noticing the unpleasant odour of the coin reminiscent of metal.

Front   *Back*

The intelligence of the spirit world changed the flowers into a coin. The coin was apported to me as an encouragement to continue my work as a medium. The coin is my treasure; it is sacred to me and will always be remembered that it was a gift from the spirit world.

We are never alone, although sometimes we feel that we are. Our life has a plan, and there is a reason why we are here, and there are many reasons as there are people for the reason we are here.

When you have those quiet moments, sit in the silence and speak to the spirit world.

They are real. There is no death. We are so loved. Listen to the quiet whispering voice, the thoughts that are not your thoughts and speak with them. Walk through the gateway and have those wonderful conversations with heaven.

Beloved Spirit Friend, Guide and Teacher

We all have our own spirit, friend and guide. If only we could be aware of their love, guidance and wisdom, we would be happier and more content in our lives. We would make better decisions and be wiser about situations that present themselves to us. For very, many years, I believed that all my thoughts were exactly that, my thoughts!

Sometimes I did wonder, however, how I knew things or sensed situations and upcoming events. I thought it was just a natural ability of mine. Then I began to realise later that some of the thoughts I had were not mine. That is to say, I would be thinking about something such as what I was going to cook for dinner that evening when another thought suddenly came into my mind about something I was not thinking about. It was as if I was talking to myself in my thoughts. I seemed to have very busy conversational thoughts - and was answering myself back. Or so I thought!

We were living in Joondalup, Western Australia. It is a beautiful area with lots of housing developments, shopping malls and businesses building up. The houses were mainly one level with lots of space and land. There were new schools and several universities in the surrounding areas. I had to travel quite a distance for work, and so before leaving the house, I enjoyed a couple of cups of tea. I always tried to ensure there was enough milk in the fridge for my morning cuppa, but sometimes the children enjoyed a drink of milk, leaving me without milk for my tea.

After work, my husband and I decided to do a mid-week shop. The shopping trolley soon filled up with the children's favourite foods. I cooked dinner whilst my husband put the shopping away. Later that evening, as I opened the fridge door, I noticed there was no milk.

We must have forgotten to get the milk.

I went to bed fed up as yet again no morning tea. Then a thought form came to me that there was milk in the back of the fridge. I disregarded my thoughts and went to bed.

The following morning as I approached the kitchen, I heard the thought-form.

"You will know I am real when you find the milk at the bottom right of the fridge at the back".

Well, I thought, that's a strange place to put a bottle of milk.

I went straight to the place where my thought communication took me, and just as was said, there at the back of the fridge, behind a stack of fresh vegetables, was a bottle of milk. I was amazed.

"Now you know I am real."

As the years have progressed, I am now well aware of my wise friend's communication with me. I can now mostly understand the difference between his words and my thoughts, although sometimes I am aware of a blending of communication. Sometimes he starts the communication, and I finish the sentence and vice versa. Sometimes he works with feelings. Often I just have a knowing about something or can feel whether a decision is good or not so good. I am of the understanding that although my wise friend is not always with me, there is definitely a positive influence.

I am grateful for my wise friend and that I am able to consciously receive his communication.

If we can be quiet in our thoughts, block out external noise, and relax totally, we may become aware of a wise friend who is inspirational and wise and is there to help and support us at all times.

Other Worldly Visitors

It had been only a few weeks since I experienced the apparition of Jacqueline in my bedroom at night that another phenomenon occurred.

Yet again, I was woken up during the night, only on this occasion, I was aware of the time. It was between 6.30, and 7.00 am. It was still very dark at this time of the morning, and the sun had yet to rise. I set my clock to 7.30 am to get everyone up for work and school.

I am not sure what had woken me up, although I was fully awake and alert when I awoke. Something or someone had woken me up. I looked across the dark unlit room, again wondering why I had been woken. I sat up in bed, wondering and sensing that there was someone in the room. All of a sudden, I became aware of the most brilliant white light that filled the bedroom.

The light was so very bright that I could not look at it and had to shield my eyes. The source of the light appeared to be at the bottom of the bed.

I tried to see through the light, which was inordinately bright; it could not possibly have been a torch or a light bulb but was piercingly white and filled the bedroom. The light then seemed to become not so bright, as if someone knew it was hurting my eyes. I tried to wake my husband, who was sound asleep, so he could see it too. But he did not stir and was completely oblivious to what I was experiencing. There seemed to be movement within this bright light, but I could not see what it was.

I was also aware of a communication taking place, but I could not hear or make sense of it. I had the feeling that I was being asked to accompany someone to go somewhere, but I didn't know with whom or where to. It was at that time that I began to get scared. I immediately turned away. The very bright light I had seen started to diminish quickly until the room was as dark as it was before the light came. I felt confused. A part of me wished I had said yes to whatever was being asked of me or to have accompanied them wherever they wanted to. I also felt annoyed with myself that I had become scared. There is something frightening about the unknown but then again the only way to discover information about the unknown is to face it. I realised there was absolutely no basis for which I should have been scared. I am waiting, however, for this to happen again, if it ever will, and decided that I would say yes next time.

I mentioned what I had experienced to my husband, who could not really understand what I was saying. I made him make a promise that whenever he felt me nudge him, he would wake up immediately.

Just to satisfy my own curiosity, I went out into the back garden next to my bedroom to scrutinise the area. I looked closely at the land, the windows and the whole area for any signs of what might have created this incredible white light. There was nothing. Where we lived had plenty of land, and not too far from the bedroom window were grape vines and fruit trees. There were no neighbours in close proximity.

The interesting phenomena remains a mystery to me. Maybe you have had a similar experience, maybe you know about these things.

What I can say is that there is nothing I know of that could have created such a bright light out of the darkness in my bedroom. I also know that I did not need to be sacred at all.

In fact, I would say I was very privileged to have had this experience.

Section Three: Communication from Spirit Family

The Truth Must be Told

"And I love you too."

It was 1998, and my beloved father had been diagnosed with terminal cancer. It was too late, and there was nothing they could do as secondary cancer had spread into his liver. They did not know where the primary cancer was. His physical strength was depleted, and it was taking all the remaining strength he had, in short bouts, to quickly talk and breathe. My mother and I kept a 24-hour vigil at the hospital, between us.

It was mom who was at the hospital on dad's final night with us when she tried to call me on the telephone. I was so tired I did not hear the phone ring, and neither did the children, so mom took a taxi home to collect me so I could be at the hospital with herself and dad. Dad was in trouble! He was now fighting for his life. I immediately woke the children and said we needed to call my aunt, who said she would look after the children and not to worry about the time because she understood the situation. It was about 3 am, but mom was reluctant to call Evelyn at such an early time. As I stood by the dining room cupboard door, I suddenly sensed my father standing next to me, and I heard him say, "your mother's never here when I need her." I then insisted we call Evelyn and quickly got the children into the car. As we dropped the children off, I had to insist that we leave immediately as it was important to get to the hospital quickly. We finally got to the hospital around 7 am, only to be told that dad had passed away 10 minutes ago. I wanted to go straight to his bed, but they asked us to wait while they tidied him up.

I felt cheated that I could not go directly to him. I did not care whether he looked tidy or not. He must have fought hard to stay here if they felt the need to hold us back for a while.

I just wanted to go to him.

Finally, we were allowed to see him.

He looked peaceful, but I could see from his expression that he had been gasping for air at the end. Mom was distraught.

She would not go near him but stood at the end of the hospital bed in shock. Suddenly she called the nurse.

"He's alive, he's still alive". I turned to look at dad, and indeed it appeared that he was trying to jump-start the body, using his knowledge of jump-starting a car as he had done many times in the past. I could see his energy field desperately trying to bring life back into the body.

Unfortunately, the body had collapsed and could no longer host his spirit. Dad was always a fighter right to the end. He never gave up on anything. As I stood close on his left side, I held his wrist with my left hand and my right on his shoulder. As I did so, I clearly spoke out, "I love you, dad." Suddenly I saw before me a blue gaseous hue outlining the contours of dad's physical body.

His spirit formed lips and spoke to me silently saying "and I love you too". It was the most amazing experience to behold. I knew then, absolutely, that we are so much more than this physical existence that we believe is our reality. We are so much more than our physical body. I then knew and understood without any doubt, from my own personal experience through the death of my beloved father, that it is our spirit which is life, not the body. Without a spirit, there can be no life. The body is empty, like an avatar. It is our spirit that uses the body as a vehicle of expression to learn and to express itself.

That very same evening, we were all in shock and totally exhausted, and when I went to sleep, it was as if I was in the very deepest of sleep.

During the night, I was woken up when it felt as if someone had struck a match and lit it under my nose. There was no way I could have slept when this happened. When I woke up, the room was dark and quiet. I looked towards the bedroom door, and I could sense that my dad was standing by the door. I said, "is that you, dad"? I tried to focus deeply on the door and sat there for quite a while, waiting to hear a reply or confirmation of some kind. I knew dad was there, and I needed him to know that I could not hear or see him. So I shrugged my shoulders as high as I could and indicated with my hands that I could not hear or see him, but I could sense him. Eventually, being so very tired, I lay back down and fell to sleep. Then dad came to me in my dream state and I had the most amazing experience. My spirit was taken temporarily to accompany my dad, and the next thing I was aware of was standing in what seemed to be a Court of Law.

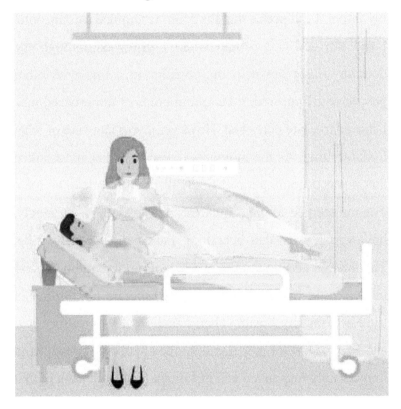

I had been asked if I would take notes of the proceedings along with a row of other people who were doing the same. I sat near a doorway which I was told I could not go through. Not because it was wrong or forbidden but because I would be unable to function or return if I did, but there was nothing stopping me from going through. I noticed a man go through a set of swinging doors with papers and other documentation, and as he went in, I tried to peep through the doorway. As I did so, I became aware of my dad. He was appealing or complaining or possibly both and I was aware that dad was there appealing or complaining and demanding to know why he was here so soon. Although I could not see my father, I did notice that the room resembled a courtroom. I did not see any people when I glimpsed through the doorway. I sat down in the corridor in a line with other people who appeared to be taking notes of the proceedings. I started to write notes fast. However, I was unaware of what I was writing. As the moments ticked by, I began to notice that it was becoming increasingly difficult for me to breathe. The air seemed to gain thickness and heaviness. Strangely, however, it was also becoming increasingly comfortable. The air was getting thicker and heavier by the moment, and now I could hardly draw breath. Desperate to continue, I tried holding my breath. Then I realised I was suffocating, and I called out for help. I caught the attention of a lady who immediately responded and instantaneously I was out of that environment and in an office which had plenty of light and fresh air. As soon as I drew my breath, I wanted to return, but I was not allowed to. I understood that I could make an appointment to return. I agreed immediately, but the appointment would not be until Wednesday, and today it was only Monday. There was nothing I could do, so I agreed to the Wednesday morning (at the time of writing it has been over 22 years and still 2 days have not elapsed in spirit world time. As I walked out of the office onto the street, I was back in bed at home with a package of knowledge that needed to unfold concerning what had been discussed when I was supposedly taking notes.

I told my mother about my "dream". The following day mom said she wanted to go and see the doctor and let him know that dad had passed away. Mom invited me to join her. At this point, I suddenly became aware that the truth must be told, and this would be the time.

I knew I had to be strong for dad but also aware not only for dad but for others too. I knew that what needed to be said would not be complimentary and I was going to need courage and strength from within to deliver whatever was going to come from my lips. All I was aware of was that the truth must be told. The doctor needed to hear the exact words from spirit. I just needed to convey the information I received from my experience, which was now, suddenly beginning to clarify into an uncanny knowing and understanding.

The conversation with my dad's towards my mother felt cold and uncaring; he showed no compassion in his response and almost appeared somewhat arrogant. Dismissively he coldly thanked her for telling him that her beloved husband had passed. Then mom turned to me and asked me if I wanted to say anything. I had the impression mom wanted me to thank the doctor for his help. But the words took over me as I spoke the voice of the spirit world. I thought, here goes... awkward ...but it's not about me, it is about something much bigger and greater than me. I felt an interesting and strange support of warm calming energy urging me forward from the spirit world as I firmly relayed the exact words that the spirit world wanted the doctor to hear. As the words of spirit were spoken they wanted me to convey to the doctor that my "father blamed him for not picking up the problem, that he had complained many times of his condition and had sought medical assistance for which he did not receive any help, advice or pain-killing medication." I was aware that my words were paused, maybe for some kind of response. Then I was encouraged to continue.

"That dad totally blamed him for not picking up the very clear signs of cancer, further, that he suffered without pain killer up until the last few days leading to his death". Even after my words the spirit world still held me in a calmness and gave me the feeling of gratitude for speaking the truth from the world of spirit. We all sat for a moment in silence. Then the doctor became angry at what I had said and grabbed my father's medical notes stating that my father had not been to the doctor in the past but had only seen him in the last month or so. I knew this to be untrue, and even my mother raised her eyebrow at this mistaken response. He held out my dad's medical notes as if to show me, but as I went to look at them, he immediately retracted them. The doctor seemed angry and agitated and even more arrogant than before. I told the doctor that I had to tell him this, no matter how unpleasant it was for us all. We left the surgery shortly after that.

A week later, mom tried to book an appointment with the doctor only to discover that he had gone off on stress leave. Mom found out that dad had not been the only patient who the doctor had missed the signs of cancer and that he had missed it many times, including his sister, who had also passed away from cancer. The doctor remained on stress leave even six months later, and I am not sure how long after that. To my knowledge the doctor did not return to work at that particular surgery.

The spirit world love us. They don't want us to suffer. They want us to experience life. I believe the spirit world needed to prevent any more unnecessary suffering. They were simply trying to correct a problem or highlight a learning to that particular doctor.

It was difficult for me to have said what needed to be said. I spoke the words as gently as I could but also with firmness.

I bless the doctor as it must have been excruciating to have heard the word of spirit, which takes no prisoners. May he now be aware in his work that the decisions he makes are known throughout the dimensions as we all are?

We are all responsible for the decisions we make, not only towards our own life, but more importantly how we respond to the needs of others, especially when we are in a position of perceived authority or greater knowledge that may affect another.

Our beloved spirit world continues to help and guide us, teaching us sometimes hard lessons.

This experience has made me aware that we have to be responsible for our actions and decisions and always aim for the greater good. My blessing to the doctor.

Funeral Date

Happy times such as weddings, birthdays, and other celebrations often bring loved ones close to us, and they, too, come close to participating in celebrations of love, joy, and happiness. Equally, in times of great support, they draw close to those who are terminally ill as well as family members. It has been recorded many times before passing that a patient will become aware of family members and friends who have passed before them and the pleasant conversations and feelings experienced from this.

Mom had been taken ill, unable to eat, and with severe stomach pain. Not only did she have dementia and alzheimer's, but also cancer in the abdominal area. After approximately three weeks in hospital to stabilise the pain and discomfort, mom returned home with the support of the MacMillan nurses and a care package. The lounge was rearranged to become her bedroom with all the equipment needed supplied. At first, mom seemed quite chirpy and was eating soft food such as yoghurt, cups of tea, water, etc., until she stated, "please, no more food"! So it was just regular sips of fluids from this moment onwards.

I would sit all day with mom, talking and sometimes singing, which made her laugh as my singing voice did not sound much like the song. We watched her favourite films and musicals together. Mom loved her home and was very much at ease despite her illness.

44

I heard a female voice tell me, "she's dying". It seemed harsh and unwanted, but it was true, and I had to accept this fact. It was around the end of August when I heard my father's voice. He gave me the date of 22 October. He said, "22 October, don't cry."

As the weeks went by, stronger morphine patches were provided. One shoulder at a time. There was even more pain-killing medication if needed.

It was around two to three days prior to mom's passing that I began to notice a change. It was as if the environment of the room had changed; the energy was different. Perhaps it was because mom was moving closer to passing, or maybe it was the universe preparing to accept mom into a new dimension of being? During this time, I hardly ever left the room. I placed a mattress on the floor at the foot of her bed so I could hear her breathing and attend to her when needed.

It was on that third night, and as I lay on the mattress, I suddenly woke up. I became aware of yet another change. Something was about to happen. I got up to look at mom, but she was sleeping peacefully, but then I noticed her breathing started to become laboured. There were pauses in her breath in-take as if it was difficult to breathe in. I reassured mom and gently moistened her lips with tepid water. Suddenly I was aware of the iciest chill I had ever experienced. The room turned to ice, and mom took her last breath. I could almost see my breath as I breathed out into the room. I looked at mom's expression and noticed a slight but definite smile. Someone she loved had come to collect her. She was released. No more pain, no more worries, just a world of love. Their gain was my loss.

The room remained as cold as ice for many hours. I made a prayer over the lifeless body of my mother and also requested whoever was around to please give me a sign that my mom was in the arms of those who loved her and that she was OK.

The undertakers arrived a couple of hours later, and it made me realise that our soul, our spirit is very much separate from the body it inhabits.

My husband had joined me a week prior to mom's passing. I asked him if he would pop up the road and buy some boxes of chocolates for the nurses who attended to mom. Meanwhile, I went onto the computer to inform the family that mom had passed peacefully into the spirit world on this day. When my husband returned, he placed a plastic carrier bag with several boxes of chocolates on the handle of the dining room door just in front of the computer which I was using. He then went upstairs.

As I continued to sit at the dining room table writing emails, I heard a rustle. It attracted my attention, but then it stopped. I continued writing when it happened again, and I thought I saw the plastic carrier bag move. Oh no, I thought, there must be a mouse somewhere. I very slowly and quietly got up from behind the computer and carefully walked towards the door with the plastic bag on it. If there was a mouse, I wanted to be sure to catch it somehow. I slowly looked behind the door but saw nothing. I gently stepped back and stood very still to see if I could see what was causing the rustle when all of a sudden, the plastic carrier bag containing boxes of chocolates swung hard on the handle of the door. There could be no mistake as the bag swung 180 degrees backward and forwards. I was amazed. This was my sign that the spirit world had responded to my request and that my mom had arrived safely into the spirit world and was in the arms of those who loved her. I immediately prayed and thanked the spirit world for honouring my request.

But what about the date given of 22 October? It was only 2 October. I now needed to find a time and date for the funeral. I preferred a Spiritual Minister to conduct the funeral. However, the funeral directors were very slow with appointments which meant that my Spiritual Minister would not be available. The only date available was 22 October! This was the date my beloved deceased father had given me several weeks prior!

How did they know this date? It seems they are aware of the past, the present, and the future.

From my experience, the world of spirit is never wrong. It is only us in the physical dimension that may misinterpret or misunderstand, but my experience is they have always been correct and have never given me untrue information.

What's It Like up there, Dad

Spirit communication for some people can often be when the mind is most settled, most relaxed. Usually, this time is when we are asleep or in a lucid dream-like state. Most of my spirit communication conveyed in this book has come to me in this way.

My beloved father had passed away from cancer some months previously when he came to visit me in my lucid dream-like state. I found myself in a very bright sunny environment. There were no clouds or sky, and neither was there any ground upon which to stand. Yet here I was, standing firmly but suspended. Dad looked well, as if he was in his prime of life, happy and healthy, very much better compared with the worn pained expression from the years and months of suffering with cancer before his passing. As I continued to observe my surroundings, I began to notice that there was, in fact, a cloud beneath our feet that seemed to be dispersing as a mist beneath me. I am not sure whether this was provided for my benefit. I was not aware of anyone else. Just me, my dad, silence and an interesting environment.

I noticed my dad kept rather a distance from me, but his smile was loving in the way that I remember him.

I asked him, "what's it like up there"? This was his reply.

"That I cannot tell you, not because I can't, but you don't have the capacity to fully understand, but it is something like this. Consider here (pointing to the right) there is a box of spare parts, arms, legs, etc., and there is a man, a crude man, but this man can do wonderful things, really wonderful things, and he puts these spare parts together.

Then consider there is a bit of this to go with it". Dad pointed to a planet, a large ball of light that had power. "Then you combine these".

"This is the nearest I can explain to you, but it is nothing like that, really."

It would appear from my spirit communication that mankind does not have the capacity to understand the immenseness of existence and we can only be left to wonder when we look through the Gateway to the Wonders of the Spirit World.

Do you have any theories about our existence on life? Do you have any thoughts as to why we are all here, living on the planet earth and what happens to us when we transition this life? Mankind has pondered about this since the dawn of time.

Magic in the Garden

A garden has always been a magical place. The magic of nature and how it can grow from seemingly nothing, beautiful flowers, shrubs, and trees. The magical colours of nature, the different shades of green, yellow, red, brown and purple and many more wonderful vibrant flowers, not to forget the beautiful fragrances that radiate from these magical forms of life. Nature has a pulse, a life force of its own. I remember being on holiday, and I was standing next to a banana tree, and I could hear the banana growing. It sounded like a buzzing pulse. The banana grew about an inch a day.

Many stories have been told about pixies and elves in the garden, and secret friends that children talk to that others cannot see. Fanciful minds and vivid imagination is what is often said to children who have invisible friends. But then we do have to consider the logic of the magic and power it takes to grow flowers, vegetables and fruits that sustain human life.

We are God's gardeners, and without trimming and pruning, the garden would soon become wild with weeds, thickets and thorns.

Have you ever camped out in a tent in the middle of a forest?

Have you ever taken a midnight walk through a nature park with a torch or lantern and become aware that there are sounds in nature that you were not aware of? Shapes and movement, rustles and cracks that can suddenly make you want to run back to camp. And what about thunder storm? How exciting it can be to listen to when we are all safe and sound.

Well, maybe there is more magic that takes place in the garden than we can ever imagine.

The whole family had gathered for the weekend during the summer holidays at grandma and grandads' house. The children were so excited to see their grandma and grandad. They were always spoiled and could do no wrong. We had woken up quite early on the Saturday morning, planning what we would be doing for the weekend. There was much hustle and bustle around the breakfast table, each of the children asking for something different and special. Grandma was only too happy to accommodate their gastronomic delights, even if it was a piece of chocolate for breakfast. There were no rules and grandma and grandad's.

"Christine, I want to show you something," said dad. "Come with me down to the garden. I want you to see something". I casually walked down the narrow garden path that ran alongside the tall right-hand side fence that backed onto the driveway which led to the garages at the back of the houses. Even though it was summer, the early morning brought a slight chill.

"Well, what have you noticed"? I looked around casually to where we had stopped, right near the small shed. I didn't notice anything different and began to wonder what it was I was supposed to be looking for. "Look this side, here at the side of the shed." As I looked, I noticed a deep hole, maybe around 4 ft, where there were carefully placed border bricks that encased a now deep empty hole.

"Ah, you have moved the tree, dad. Where did you move it to? I can't see it in the garden," I replied. "I haven't touched the tree. It just disappeared. It was here a few days ago, and then as I was walking down the pathway, I noticed it was gone. It would have taken a few strong men to move that tree. Have a look around the garden and see if you can find it because I can't find it. I cannot believe it has just disappeared. Who would want to take that tree"? Dad mused. I looked around the garden, but the tree was not to be found. "How strange. Are you sure you didn't move it"? "I could not have moved that tree even if I wanted to. It would have been too big and heavy for me to move. I cannot understand how it was moved because there is a lot of soil that has gone with it also." "Well, I suppose there is not much we can do about it. It's gone, and that's that"! It was certainly rather puzzling, to say the least.

"There's a lot of funny stuff going on in this garden. I dare not tell your mother because I think she would be quite scared". We slowly walked back to the house in wonderment and disbelief that a big heavy tree would have gone missing. We soon forgot about the mystery as the laughter and playfulness of the children commanded our attention.

We had a wonderful weekend of strawberry picking and going to car boot sales, and sitting together around the dinner table talking about what we had bought. Just as we were leaving on Sunday evening, I made arrangements to return in a couple of weeks' time.

With work and organising the children, the two weeks seemed to move quickly, and soon we were packing our belongings again and getting the car ready to visit grandma and grandad for the weekend. The journey seemed a long three hours' drive as the traffic was heavy during the late afternoon. We had a light evening meal, and the children were soon asleep in bed.

"You hoo, it's a lovely morning. Are you getting up?" I heard my mother's voice in the garden. Mom loved to get up early and enjoy a cup of tea in the garden whilst walking around the garden looking at the flowers. I could also hear the children in the garden playing with their grandmother. Mom was obviously hoping I would get up soon and help her out with the children. I climbed out of bed and got myself dressed and ready for the day when I realised it was 5.30 am. I was secretly hoping I could have stayed in bed until at least 7.30 am. I walked into the sun lounge, which backed on the garden with its big windows, only to discover my mom and dad and older daughter sitting in front of the television with a small heater on. Everyone was still in their bedclothes. "Oh, so you have come back in the house then"? They all gave me a puzzled look. "What do you mean, darling?" Said, dad. "I heard you outside calling me to get up, so I'm up. It suddenly dawned on me that perhaps nobody had been in the garden.

"You have been in the garden, haven't you"? "No, we have only just got up. We are not dressed yet. It's a bit too chilly to go outside in the garden yet". "But, that's strange, I heard you calling my name, and I heard the children too"! I would always be able to recognise the children's voices as well as my mother's voice. I looked out of the window to see if the neighbour was up, but nobody was in the garden, and it was only 5.30 am after all. How strange, very puzzling. When the rest of the family finally came downstairs for breakfast, my dad said, "follow me. I want to show you something."

We walked down the garden and yet again stopped at the shed.

"Look at this. I cannot believe it".

We had stopped at the place where a couple of weeks ago, a huge hole had been left from the uncanny disappearance of a very large old tree. As I looked at this spot in the garden, the very large old tree with all its soil had returned, just as if it had never been moved. Both me and dad just stared in disbelief. It certainly would have taken a couple of strong men and a hoist to have moved that tree. "Why is it back"? I asked dad. "Why did it disappear, and how did it reappear"? Even to this day, it is a mystery that has not been solved.

There is much magic in the garden , sometimes it is only the avid gardeners who know their garden well, that can tell an uncanny story.

Forests and woods hold many secrets too. There is a communication of nature when in a forest or wood that can be felt. Some say it is healing and they always feel invigorated after a walk in the woods or forest. Others feel wary as they are very aware of the sounds, clicks and cracks from branches, the sound of rustling leaves and perhaps acorns that seemingly drop on one's head, as well as the fragrance of the soils, barks and fauna. Some believe that messages and prayers are stronger in the forests, that messages and requests can be communicated through the magical essence of nature itself.

What are your thoughts?

Asportation and Apportation in the Garage

I was so proud to have my own first car. It was a Ford Escort. I loved my car, and my father said he would give it a service for me over the pit in his garage. My father had an engineering mind and loved to work with mechanical engines. Dad used to get quite frustrated from time to time, saying he couldn't find his tools and that he knew he had put them in a particular place, and now they had gone. He used to get very fed up and end up walking away, locking his garage up behind him. This time would be no different, except there were witnesses.

My dad, myself, and a friend were standing around the front of the car. The bonnet was up, and we were learning about the functions of each piece of the engine. Dad continued to explain, and I learned a lot from his casual, easy-going mechanical teachings. Dad then went to the workbench and picked up a tool to use in the engine. He continued explaining whilst using the tool. None of us had moved. We were all looking in the engine when my dad said, "Can anyone see where I put the tool"? We gazed at where dad had been working, but none of us could see the tool. "Don't move," said dad. "It can only be at arm's length as none of us have moved from where we are standing". Carefully we examined all around the engine, around the sides, and then on the floor. The tool was nowhere to be found. Making sure that my friend and I did not move, he took a few steps towards the workbench, just in case! The tool was nowhere to be found. Strangely relieved, dad said, "Thank goodness I have got witnesses to this. I thought I was going around the bend." I drove the car out of the garage and parked it up. All three of us then looked in the garage for the tool for quite some time. Dad was always in the garage working. He kept it very organised and squeaky clean. It was about 3 weeks later, when dad went into the garage, he heralded that the tool had turned up. "I just walked up to the bench, and there was the tool, sitting in the middle, on its own."

I have heard of people who have experienced this type of phenomenon and thought of themselves as going around the bend. It is fortunate that my dad had witnesses to this phenomenon. Some call it poltergeist activity, others may give it another name. But for me, it is a phenomenon that would warrant genuine scientific research, for this could help humanity understand aspects of life and energy that is mainly untapped.

Unfortunately, the disappearances and reappearances continued through the rest of his life, but he felt comfortable in the fact that others knew what was happening. He always told me that there were a lot of strange things that were happening and if he told them all, we would be quite frightened.

What are your thoughts about this type of phenomenon? Do you often inexplicably loose items and then they seem to magically turn up at a later date, sometimes in the place you have previously looked or somewhere quite strange?

Section Four: Phenomena Around Us

Unexplained Clanging at the Joondalup Consultation Rooms

There are unseen forces around us all of the time. It would seem that the energies around us are varied with different levels of power. Some forces we can attune to easily others are not so easy. Below is an example of an unexplained powerful force which was experienced by myself and a colleague.

I was operating my own healing practice in a business centre in Joondalup. There were about 20 different businesses each renting their own consulting room. We all knew each other well and often gave each other advice where possible. I would often walk around the building to check if anyone wanted to have any healing in between my clients. Sometimes when we were just chatting over a cup of tea, I would be asked if I would place my hands on someone's shoulders for pain relief, relaxation or a top up in energy.

One evening after my evening meal at home, I received a phone call from a paraplegic colleague at the business centre. My colleague was in distress and in pain and asked if I could immediately help him. It seemed as if I had not long left the centre after working a long day, but I agreed. I would not be able to return until around 11 pm. My colleague agreed, he just needed help. I arrived at the centre to discover him already waiting outside in his car. After switching all the alarms off and putting on the lights we went directly to my healing room. He was distraught. He was in pain and seemed emotionally frail. It was a very hot evening so before we started I wedged my door open and opened the back door of the centre again wedging it with a brick to allow the flow of cool air.

I set to work immediately. I had been working on my colleague for around half an hour when I became aware of strange sounds as we conducted a visualisation of moving the pain out of his body. The sounds became a loud clanging which was undeniable as it reverberated loudly throughout the centre, shaking the building. The clanging sounded like metal on metal. The building did not have central heating radiators or fire extinguishers. We were both rather shocked. As my client was a paraplegic I decided to go to the back door to investigate the undeniable occurrence. There was nothing obvious. At this point there was no further clanging. The building suddenly seemed quiet and peaceful. Only the occasional gentle breeze could be felt. We both became alarmed and unsure of what was taking place. My colleague decided he wanted to leave the building immediately and suggested we meet in our respective cars in a car park some distance from the building. He also suggested we tell someone what we had experienced and so asked me if I would follow him home to tell his wife. My client was visibly and emotional disturbed by the turbulence in the building at that time I knew the family well but was rather reluctant as it was now 1.00 am. Reluctantly I agreed. Suddenly there was another continuous sound of crashing and clanging of metal in the building. The whole building shook. It was so loud I put my hands over my ears. There were no fire extinguishers, there was no metal and the building was locked. There was only the two of us in the building which stood on a large piece of land away from any other building. I too, then decided it was time to go, quickly! I went to the back door which opened to a private court yard to close and lock up when again another loud banging of metal, so loud I again wanted to put my hands over my ears. When I returned to my healing room and my client who had now returned into his wheelchair, I noticed that some papers looked as if they had been messed up on my desk. My colleague was frightened and the colour had drained from his face. Neither of us had had an experience of this type before. I began to tremble. My colleague wanted to get away as fast as possible. There was no logical sense to this loud metallic banging. I confirmed that yes, we ought to leave right now. I further told my colleague to show no fear and to carefully make his way to the car and I would lock up and reset the alarm. We both made our way to our car. I was amazed how quickly he managed to pack his wheelchair and have the car engine running ready to do a 'get away'. I quickly set the alarm locked up and jumped into my car and we drove away to the car park where we stopped to discuss what we thought was happening, but we had no explanation I subsequently followed him home where we continued to discuss our experience over a cup of tea. It didn't seem that I stayed long at all, but when I arrived home, I noticed it was gone 3.00 am.

I decided I was too tired to return to the Centre the following morning, so rescheduled my clients. It was three days later that I returned to the Centre. When I walked toward the building, as I stepped over the threshold, I said internally, loudly and firmly and with a feeling of authority, "I'm back"! I noticed as I approached the reception area that all the doors and windows of the building were open. I asked the young lady on reception why all the doors and windows were open. She said that for the last three days there had been a terrible smell in the building. They did not know where it was coming from and they couldn't get rid of it. I said, well you can close them now, it won't come back (and it didn't). She then informed me that she needed to contact my colleague because he would not return to the Centre unless I was there first.

I walked into my room and noticed that my books were off the shelves and my papers were scattered all over the floor and desk. I know this was not the way I had left my room the other night. It was about twenty minutes later that my colleague arrived. We had a good chat. We tried to find out what it was that caused that incredible clanging sound in the building, but we never did. It certainly wasn't anything physical from this world.

There was no seismic activity reported anywhere in the area or remotely. To this day I have no rational explanation for the strange experience and the fact that somebody else experienced it also reinforces the occurrence and my evidence of the phenomenon. There is a power, a universal power, that exists around us. Perhaps one day mankind will fully understand our environment differently and be able to tap into this universal power. Have you had any similar experiences?

The Magic of Telepathy

A Town Called Elliot

Is there such a phenomenon as telepathic communication? Some people say yes, and some people would disagree, but this story strongly indicates that there is such communication as the phenomenon of telepathy.

It was Christmas time in Australia, and living in the Northern Territory at this time of the year, the heat was stifling. And my four young school-aged children and I were living and working in central northern territory in a small town called Elliot. Elliot comprised a small school, hotel, post office, garage, small church and two aboriginal tribes geographically placed apart on either side of the hotel.

It was the end of term, the school had closed to students, and all the tidying up had been done.

Some of the teachers had already left to take time in a cooler climate by moving south to Melbourne, Adelaide and other territories. My mother had just arrived from the United Kingdom, having flown initially to Sydney where we had relatives and then travelling on the Ghan train to Adelaide and then journeying by coach from Adelaide to Elliot. Mom arrived at Elliot around 7 am. It was very hot and almost impossible to stand outside in the terrific heat without being half eaten alive by mosquitoes and flies. Mom was excited to have finally arrived at the destination with her daughter and four grandchildren. It had been a very long journey, and she was tired. When she arrived at our small teacher bungalow, which comprised two bedrooms, a bathroom/laundry/walk-in shower and a lounge and kitchen area, we made tea/breakfast. It was small but workable, and we would not be spending much time there anyway, as I had booked for us all to go and visit Darwin for the holidays.

For the two to three days that we had left in Elliot, we visited a disused hotel that was off the highway. History had it that it had been a very busy hotel at one time and catered for the drovers and other visitors who passed through. The local government at the time decided it was going to move the road in another direction, which meant that people did not see the hotel, and so as there were no longer any customers, the owners moved out, and it had, over the years, fallen into disrepair.

As we walked through the old hotel, which was open for anyone to see and visit, it was interesting to experience a bygone era. There was dust and sand on the floor, which had blown in over time. The old wooden bar still stood strong, and at the back, there was a smallish room with an old heater/cooker where hotel food would have been cooked. During the hot weather, it must have been stifling in that small kitchen at the back of the hotel. There were remains of a barn where horses would have rested and also a separate building with single beds, a wash bowl, a chair and what looked like the remains of an old mirror. This was where the drovers would have stayed.

The hotel had been very basic but at the time very much needed, but as always, as time moved on, everything changed. As we stood out in the front, the children were running around and playing with each other, bringing a sort of much-needed life back into the old place. As the wind gently blew, we noticed what we called a 'dust devil' blowing which is a mini vortex of wind that whips up all the sand and may last for just a couple of minutes before its energy expires. As it started to grow darker, we returned to the car and headed back to Elliot. Life had been very hard for people living in the outback years ago, living and working the land, especially in places like the northern territory where there was very little water, extreme heat and lots of hard work just to survive.

I was one of the last teachers to leave the school as we headed up north towards Darwin.

From Elliot, we passed through Dunamarra, Daly Waters, Larrimah, Mataranka, Katherine, Pine Creek and then onto Darwin, the most northerly part of the Northern Territory. It took us more than twenty-four hours to reach Darwin.

We booked into our motel occupying two rooms. It was very clean and modern with a swimming pool and sunbathing patio and was close to the Darwin shopping centre. The cooking facilities comprised several BBQs around the grounds. One afternoon an aboriginal musician and his children were looking at a cage. He beckoned to the children to "come to have a look". Curled around the outside of a birdcage was a snake. He told the children that the snake was only after his meal (a bird in the cage) then he would be gone. No one was to touch it as it was dangerous, and for a short while, he kept a vigil on the children to look but not get too close.

We headed to the local beach, but as we were heading to the water to have a paddle, a very tall seven-foot tall good-looking aboriginal male walked cautiously towards us. He spoke perfect English and informed us that it was not safe to go near the sea as there was a thirty-footer crocodile swimming very close to the shore. We stayed about half an hour and then decided to leave. We made our way back to the motel so the children could use the swimming pool and make some friends

***

At some stage during the middle of the night, something woke me up. The room was pitch black as the curtains were also black-out quality due to the hot daytime and brightness of the day. I looked around the room and could see nothing in the darkness when suddenly I looked towards the glass patio doors, which were heavily curtained with black-out material. As I looked closely, a light began to appear from the bottom of the curtain and began rising up toward the middle of the curtain. Initially I automatically assumed it was someone's car headlights shining, but then realised that this was not possible because I could see quite clearly now that the light image was that of an orangutang or a gorilla which seemed to be doing some kind of a dance raising his arms and legs on both sides of this body. As I continued to watch the image, I heard the words, "you should not have done this to Christine." As I continued to watch this dance, the image began to move up the curtain towards the ceiling and then disappeared, leaving the room in complete darkness once again. The whole experience lasted approximately 5 minutes.

The following morning I mentioned this to my mother and asked if someone was looking after her home in the UK whilst she was away. Mom assured me that her house was OK. Just then, a lady from reception knocked on the door saying that there was a telephone call for me. I went to the reception and took the call, and it was from the Elliot Police station from the small bush town where we were living.

Our bungalow had been broken into! It appeared that the incidence of the break in and horror of what had happened had instantly travelled around he world. The local Elliot Police had access all my stored landline telephone contacts asking if anyone knew my whereabouts so they could contact me. They even made a call to the Middle East.

The police had heard a lot of noise as there was music and dancing going on in the small bungalow by a group of travelling aborigines who had also taken our belongings into the bush.

As a result we decided we needed to leave and return to Elliot. When we returned, the bungalow had been trashed and was uninhabitable. I arranged for a padlock to be put on the front and back door and decided to continue to Alice Springs to enjoy the rest of our holiday. We spent the following two weeks there before mom had to return to Sydney for her flight back to the UK.

The four children and myself returned to Elliot with lots of cleaning chemicals, and we were invited to stay at the local police officer's house. The Northern Territory Education Department immediately evacuated myself and another teacher to different schools. Even after a week of cleaning, I still did not feel the small bungalow was clean enough to live in. I decided to move away from Elliot, and we were moved to Alice Springs. The day before we left, Elliot, one of the female elders, came to visit me.

"Did you get our message? We tried to message you about what happened to your bungalow." I immediately remembered the image on the inside of the thick heavy curtain at the motel. This was the image the local Elliot people had sent to me to warn me about what was happening inside my cottage. "Yes, I did get a message". I thanked her and the group for sending telepathically the message I had received through the animal kingdom imagery.

When I spoke to the Chief of Police, he informed me that he said, "you should not have done this to Christine". These were the exact words I heard at the motel in combination with the imagery.

There is a power, a phenomenon that we are not, at this moment in time, able to fully understand, but it is part of us as spiritual beings, our human heritage. It has always been with us, but for some reason, we have forgotten how to use these abilities. Slowly and surely, we are now re-awakening to our true spirit.

Ancient tribes have held the knowledge safely and securely within their culture to remind us all, when the time comes, of who we truly are and our true abilities.

The Swimming Pools and Synchronicity

When there is unjustified negativity that is focused on someone, there can be an equal and opposite effect on the perpetrator.

I want to emphasise unjustified as being spiteful, uncalled for or just plain nastiness.

We meet all kinds of people in our life journey, some who stay with us for a lifetime whilst others for a season as well as those who we pass by with like ships in the night. Each encounter imprints an experience of one kind or another, which the personality of our spirit is part of.

There are many people who are at the receiving end of negative people, but take heed of those who should not be messed around with!

As a healer, I made a point of helping everyone who came to know me or needed healing. Often working without pay for those who had no money whilst still performing a professional service. I do not think ill of anyone, and I believe we are all entitled to the point of view.

However, something rather interesting took place within a period of two months which made me realise that not everyone you consider a friend always is. Spirt can be very protective.

There were two people I knew quite well. Neither of them knew of the other as they were two separate friends, as

I thought. I would occasionally meet for coffee and have a chat about anything and everything.

I had not heard from one friend for what seemed a long time, so I made contact, asking if everything was OK. I learned that my friend had had a very distressing experience. This was the story in my friend's words.

"I decided the swimming pool needed cleaning out. Petals from the flowers had got into the pool. I walked up to the edge of the pool, and somehow I fell into the pool. Not only did I fall in, but somehow I ended up at the bottom of the deep end and banged my head on the bottom. It really hurt, and as I did, so I gulped water and lost my breath. I don't know how this happened, but it was as if I was pushed.

I was in such shock when I surfaced and got out of the pool immediately. I had to rest to get my breath and bring up the water I had swallowed. I was in so much shock that I didn't go back into the garden for weeks. It took me longer still before I went anywhere near the pool. As my shock of near drowning took place, I decided to go on holiday for a couple of weeks to recover from the shock."

We can all sometimes fall into the pool, and most of us jump in, but on this occasion, it was not just the falling into the pool, it was the feeling of being pushed, losing balance and hitting the head at the bottom of the pool. My friend was a good swimmer and was used to going underwater. He just couldn't understand what had happened.

Sometime later, I caught up with another friend I had not heard from for a while. I told her I was just checking on how things were going. I was now shocked! This was the story my other friend told me.

"I decided to visit my sister, but when I got there, they were out.

I called them, and they told me they would be back within the hour and to sit in the garden next to the pool. I pulled out a sun chair and sat down but then decided that perhaps I could make myself useful and clean the pool up from some petals that were floating on the top. I walked towards the edge of the pool, and somehow I fell in and went all the way down to the bottom and hit my head at the bottom of the pool. I thought I was going to drown. It was as if I had been pushed and held down underwater.

When I surfaced, I was in shock. I was so shocked that I could not stay anywhere near the pool. I was sopping wet, yet I was determined to go home. I caught the bus home in sopping wet clothes and was in shock for weeks."

I found the synchronicity of this interesting. Both friends used the same words and had the same experience of the feeling of being pushed; both hit their heads at the bottom and felt held down at the bottom of the pool. I did discover later that they had not been such good friends as I had thought they were.

Was this a punishment from the spirit world? I was obviously expected to learn of their experience, which brought to light their individual negativity. The moral of this true story is to be careful what you say and think.

There is always someone listening!

Physical Contact from Spirit World

Some would say that the spirit world cannot touch us or interact with us. However, I know differently from my experience in life. Make your own mind up after reading the following story.

After the local school in Elliot was raided along with our bungalow, which was broken into and most of our belongings stolen, we decided to leave Elliot. With the help of the education department, we were moved to Alice Springs. I obtained a position at Alice Springs high school. For just a week or so, we stayed in a very nice motel whilst searching for a rental property. The motel was very clean and had a swimming pool as well as a patio to sit outside in the sunshine. We had a kitchenette, bathroom and five beds in the bedroom/lounge area. We were quite comfortable there for the short term as we had worked very hard cleaning up the small bungalow that had been broken into and trashed in Elliott, Northern Territory. The bungalow we left in Elliot had been badly damaged, and I had spent weeks cleaning up, repainting and making it liveable again. When the removalist lorry came to pack all of what was left of our belongings, the driver called to say he was just 2 hours away. It was now evening, and the local tribes and police were busy having to deal with the influx of several gangs of aboriginals who were rioting throughout Elliot, causing chaos, burning buildings and shooting in the streets. There was chaos, and the police were fully stretched. Reinforcement units had been drafted in.

Over the telephone, I informed the removalist driver that it was not safe for him to travel into Elliot due to the rioting and that it would be better if he could stop at a different town until morning.

He agreed, parked his lorry in a secure area and slept in the cab until the morning. He arrived around 9.30 am the following morning after checking how safe Elliot was. He worked quickly, and within an hour and a half, both the lorry, myself and the children were on the road heading for Alice Springs. The small teacher bungalow was left clean, liveable and padlocked, so entry was not possible without keys.

Elliot lost all its teachers that year except for the Principal and his wife. The three other teachers were relocated to other separate northern territory schools.

It must have been very difficult for the Principal and his wife to run the whole school on their own until the beginning of the following term as the recruitment process was rather slow. The journey from Elliot to Alice Springs being around 762 km took us about 7 hours and it was late afternoon when we finally arrived in the Motel organised by the education department.

It had been a very hot sticky day and as soon as we arrived at the motel, we all quickly found our swimming costumes and headed directly to the swimming pool. The evening gave no relief to the relentless heat. As the children sat in the motel room watching television, I sat just outside the door on the patio, having a cup of tea. I started talking to a couple from London who were journalists. They were asking me questions about my work and where I had been. They seemed pleasant, but I noticed they seemed quite judgmental towards me when I mentioned why we had been relocated. They did not believe my somewhat guarded story about what had happened in Elliot. I decided enough was enough and excused myself from their company. I walked into the motel room and got the children ready for bed. The air-conditioning was on, and the children fell quickly to sleep. I sat back outside the door as it was still quite early for me to go to bed. About forty-five minutes later, as I walked into the room, I noticed Jacqueline was out of bed. I went in, and she told me she did not feel very well and that she woke up and an elderly lady with long grey, unkempt hair was standing by the side of her bed looking at her. I know that nobody had been in the motel room because I was literally just sitting outside the door. Jacqueline was quite distressed, so she sat with me for a while before she decided she would have my bed. At around 9 pm, after finished my cup of tea sitting outside looking at the clear inky blue sky and bright stars, I decided it was time to go to bed. I walked in and began to get changed into my night clothes when all of a sudden, I felt a big push from the left side of my body. The push was so strong I tripped over and ended up on the floor.

I couldn't believe I had tripped and fallen over. There was nobody except the children in the room and the door was locked. I felt rather shaken and a little shocked. I got up, brushed myself down looking around the room and checking the floor where I convinced myself that I must have slipped. After getting myself up, I went to bed. The following morning we were all up early. I took a shower and noticed that I had finger mark bruises down the left-hand side of my body where I was pushed and fell over the previous night. There was a sudden realisation. I had definitely been pushed. But by whom and why? I spoke in depth to Jacqueline about this elderly lady she saw. She said the lady was horrible and as soon as she slept in my bed, she was OK. She told me that the angry lady had gone now and she no longer felt unwell.

It was just a few days later when we finally moved into our rented property in Saddadeen, Alice Springs. The children had new schools and made friends quickly.

Some say that the spirit world is unable to interact with us in the physical world, or that those in spirit have no power in this world. However, there is much evidence to suggest that this is not necessarily so. In the case of Jacqueline and the elderly lady, Jacqueline had been feeling unwell for a couple of days, and I wonder if the elderly lady was there to help her or heal her in some way. Certainly, the following morning she was feeling well again. Was I being told off by the spirit lady for sitting outside the door early evening? Was she so angry with me that she pushed me over? Or was this a separate spirit? I wonder how many spirits were there.

There is certainly more to our world than most of us realise.

Perhaps we should be more aware of our surroundings and what is going on. Often there is too much noise in our world, such as tv, cars, trains, aircraft, music etc., to listen to the soft loving communication from the world of spirit.

We have happy memories of Alice Springs, the people and the friends we made. But it certainly was interesting regarding the spiritual activity. Alice Springs is in central Australia in the middle of the desert!

Asportation of Sunglasses

An asport is an object that is relocated from one place to another.

The object is known. Whereas an Apport is an object which is not known to the recipient and is transported through the etheric to the recipient that would have a particular meaning.

This story concerns a pair of sunglasses.

My son James and his newly wedded wife flew over from Australia to the UK in the summer holidays. It was a beautiful summer, and James was touring on holiday to fly over to Ireland but was stopping over for just a couple of nights at his grandmother's.

When he arrived, he was recounting memories of when he was a small child visiting grandma and grandad, playing in the garden and helping his grandad around the house. He had some wonderful memories but was saddened that his grandad was no longer with us.

We had made arrangements to visit some very close family friends for lunch who were looking after their elderly mother, who had dementia and Alzheimer's.

It was a beautiful drive down into the country, driving through the narrow hedged lanes and seeing the rays of sunshine streaming through the trees. There was a gentle, welcomed breeze that carried summertime fragrances. Life can feel so peaceful and beautiful this time of the year.

We had had some wonderful Christmases with Aunt Topsy, Uncle Jack, Edward and Anne. Aunt Topsy and Uncle Jack were farming people and lived in a beautiful white cottage down toward the bottom of a narrow lane in Alfrick, Worcestershire. When we went down on Christmas Eve, it always snowed, and it brought great excitement when the car was driving up and down these unlit narrow high hedged lanes. Not many people would have dared drive through these lanes in such conditions, and being late evening made the journey even more exciting. The driver had to be careful not to slip into the ditches at the side of the road, which carried a stream of water that, in some places, was quite deep. Christmas would not have been Christmas without going to the cottage. There was always a healthy hot wood fire burning when we walked in. I remember the terrific heat and how the fragrance of the wood filled the room.

This was Christmas to me. The front room was the best room and was beautifully decorated, giving a warm red-coloured aspect to the room. There was a large antique mirror on one of the walls, and I remember at the side of the fire were beautiful leather straps with horseshoes and other interesting copper pieces. As they hung down at the side of the fireside, the brightly polished copper glowed with the colour of the fire. The farm was quite large, and Uncle Jack and his sheepdog Rusty had to get up very early in the morning to fetch the sheep. There was a plum orchard and apple trees, chickens and root vegetable fields. It was a magical place for everyone with lots of laughter, happiness and joy. We lived the whole year for this moment.

But like all things, times do change. Just like the seasons of the year. Aunt Topsy and Uncle Jack eventually parted for a better world, and so the beautiful cottage we all loved so much was sold.

Edward and Anne lived in Droitwich, and we were all looking forward to getting together and having a good chat over lunch. The day was filled with happiness and laughter, and like all good times, it always passed too quickly. After a wonderful day, we began our way home. James and his wife would be leaving for Ireland early the following morning, so were keen to pack and ensure their passports were easily accessible. Not long after we arrived the telephone rang. It was Edward. He had noticed a pair of sunglasses on the coffee table, which did not belong to them and said they must belong to James. James checked, and yes, he realised he had left his sunglasses behind.

Edward suggested that he could put them in the post, but James declined to say that he could easily buy another pair and not to bother forwarding them. They would not have arrived before their flight to Ireland in any case.

Later that evening, I was looking for my car keys and decided that I must have left them in my handbag. I began fumbling about in my handbag, unable to locate my car keys and realised that I needed to tip everything out of my bag onto the armchair just to check what was actually in my bag! As I was going through the items, I noticed a pair of sunglasses that did not belong to me.

"Does anyone recognise these sunglasses?" I asked quizzically.

James took a look and said, "Oh, those are mine. I thought I had left them at Edwards. Thanks, mom, that saves me buying another pair".

I quickly called Edward back, saying that James had indeed got his sunglasses and that the ones on the coffee table must have belonged to someone else.

When I spoke to Edward, I asked him if he still had the sunglasses. He said they had been moved somewhere. He placed the handset down temporarily to look for the sunglasses, and they were not to be seen. "I don't understand it, they were here earlier on, and nobody moved them; how strange". Edward never found the sunglasses that were left on the coffee table, but strangely James had them returned in a mysterious manner.

Stranger things happen in life compared to fiction. Was the pair of sunglasses asported into my bag? Was it any coincidence that I was looking for my car keys (which I found) in my handbag prior to James leaving for Ireland? What were the circumstances that enabled this transportation of sunglasses from one place to another? Whatever the answer, it required power and energy to make this happen.

Have you ever wondered how or why certain objects are found in a place you would last look? Do you remember placing it there? Is it the phenomena of asportation and apportation? Sometimes it can be months or longer before objects are found.

Do you think there may be a phenomenon of asportation and apportation around your home and family too?

Absolute Love and Support from the World of Spirit

It has been my experience to learn that we are never alone in this world. There is so much love, guidance and spiritual inspiration that is constantly given to us.

If we develop our skills of listening and communicating with nature, we can draw inspiration and ideas that not only benefit mankind but also provide happiness and contentment.

Even though life can be tough, we are never alone. Our emotions, prayers and thoughts are always known to the unseen forces of nature.

* * *

It was Autumn, the skies were grey, and the rolling mists of the Beacon brought heavy showers and cold winds. My mother had now reached her later years of life and needed loving family support. I relocated to live with my mother to support and help with the cruel illness of dementia and alzheimers. Dementia is a very cruel disease, like many other diseases. It was taking away the beautiful soft loving personality and nature of my mother little by little every day. Her memories were disappearing as well as her recognition of people. Apart from the odd occasion mom recognised who I was right up to the end. The dementia was making it increasingly difficult for me to provide for her the help she so very much needed. She knew something was happening, and she could feel a change coming over her just before she experienced an outburst of illogical and difficult behaviour.

"I'm sorry, I am really sorry, really I am. I am so sorry." Mom was trying to apologise for her cruel disease, which had been diagnosed as dementia and alzheimer's. We both knew it was claiming more of her each day. My younger daughter Melanie decided to fly to the UK to spend some time with us, and I decided that it might be a good idea to book a short holiday for maybe 2 or 3 nights in Devon, which my mother loved so dearly. In years past, mom and dad had bought a caravan as a holiday home in Torbay. It was placed on a wonderful site with leisure facilities of a swimming pool and entertainment/dance floor. There were several cafes and eateries also as well as an onsite fish and chip shop and general stores. It was a very popular campsite that accommodated tents, mobile holiday vans, as well as static caravans and cottages. Every time we mentioned Devon, mom's expression would turn to joy. As we no longer had the caravan, I booked a 3-bedroom van for 3 nights. Unfortunately, it was not as successful for mom as we had hoped. As the caravan was unfamiliar, there was an inner fear that I could sense from her. She would not leave the caravan and, at night, slept on the settee. The alzheimers seemed to get worse as she began to misunderstand what bedtime meant and what the bed was for. It was just as hard on Melanie too, who became rather distraught and frustrated and told me that she wanted to go back to Australia the following day. Life was difficult for us all, as I am sure if you have experienced this type of disease in the family, the problems and difficulties are all too well known.

On return to the Midlands, I booked a flight for my daughter Melanie to return to Australia the following day. I drove Melanie to the airport with mom in the car also and helped her organise her flight back onto the emirates flight. As soon as my daughter boarded the flight, a deep feeling of despair took over me as I needed to help mom as best as I could as well as survive myself. My family were all in Australia, and I was away from the family and unknown to me at the time, I would be for quite a few years.

* * *

As well as making regular outings together, I decided that it might be good for mom to join a day club. The local community centre held a day for people to arrive to do activities, have lunch, do more activities and then return home. They could even take a supper home with them if they booked it.

There was transport available which would pick them up and return them. It sounded ideal. I arranged for mom to participate. When she came back off the small coach, she seemed very happy and lively. It seemed to be doing her a world of good, and it also gave me a day to myself. After a few weeks of this one day a week out of the house, mom decided that she no longer wanted to go. It was taking more and more persuasion to get her to the club.

On the last day that mom attended her day out, I was feeling exhausted.

I was sleep deprived, and the constant need for mental gymnastics to keep mom happy began taking its toll on my health and wellbeing. The wonderful volunteers who drove the small coach had by now realised that they needed to pick mom up last and return her first. The small coach was full of people, and the two volunteers came to collect her. Mom would not move and refused to get out of the armchair. It seemed my brief few hours for myself were about to disappear.

The gentleman volunteer persisted in persuading her but eventually reminded her that he had a small coach full of people, and they had all been waiting patiently and unfortunately, he would have to leave her. My heart dropped. I was exhausted, frustrated and in desperate need of even just two or three hours to myself. I begged him just once again that we all try. It took three of us to encourage her out of the chair, and she eventually walked slowly down the front garden path cursing me and telling me that she hated me, really hated me. It broke my heart as her expression matched her words. But deep down, I knew this was not my mother at this time; this was dementia. It was quite late in the morning by this time, and as I waved goodbye, I felt instant relief. Just for a short time, I would be able to relax, do some washing, have a cup of tea and just be myself. It was an opportunity for me to organise everything for when mom returned.

I shut the front door with a sigh of relief and headed straight for the kitchen for a cup of coffee and to decide which job I needed to do first. Tears of emotion were streaming down my cheeks, but I had to get organised.

Just as I was making a drink, I heard a loud patter on the kitchen wall cupboards. The sound stopped me in my tracks. Where did all that noise come from? Then it continued becoming increasingly loud.

The sound now became a banging not only on the cupboards but also on the wall, and then it moved to the ceiling, then into a very loud thumping on the walls and ceiling. The sound was so loud I cowered and hunched down, wondering what was happening. Just then, the phone rang. I ran out of the kitchen to pick up the phone. It was my husband from Australia. I told him what I had just experienced, and he suggested it was mom returning and banging on the front door. That would not have been anyone banging on the front door because it was too loud and was in the kitchen - nowhere near the front door.

Nevertheless, I went to the front door anyway, but of course, there was nobody there. I checked outside the kitchen, but still, nobody was there. The sound was in the kitchen, without a doubt. When I returned to the kitchen, I explained to my husband exactly what I had experienced in the kitchen and started to tap myself on the wall cupboards in an attempt to replicate the sound. I could not project the intensity of the sound or even the same tone.

What did happen, however, was there was a response to my knocking on the cupboard walls. I knocked twice, and then the knock was returned twice. I continued with three knocks, it was immediately returned with three knocks. The returned knocks were much quieter, now aligning with the intensity of my knocking.

The sounds had intelligence. There was an intelligent response. The spirit world was responding to my emotional state. I suddenly realised how blessed I was that there were intelligent beings around me and understood what my mother and myself were experiencing and the highly charged emotion that accompanied it.

That very same night, exhausted, I went to bed. Mom continued to sit in the armchair downstairs in the lounge, refusing to go to bed. As I climbed into bed, I sat up with the soft pillows supporting me, wondering how I was going to continue, when all of a sudden, I was aware of a man's voice behind the left-hand side of the back of my head. The voice was so clear it was as if someone was actually in the room behind me.

"Hello, how are ya? You'll be all right. I'm ya boyfriend. See ya soon!"

I have to this day, no idea who this 'boyfriend' was supposed to be in spirit. Again this was another acknowledgement of communication and support from the world of spirit. Although I was not too sure about the "see ya soon" bit. But I had a chuckle. Several years later, my spirit friend was correct; everything worked out well with care help and MacMillan nurses.

Never believe you are alone. Even when you are in your darkest moments, there is a love around you helping you, sympathising with you and doing everything to let you know that you are not alone and they are there with you, trying to support you, always.

Lucky Black Cat

Omens and Messengers

Our prayers are always heard

Many may associate with the feeling of 'where to now' in life. The need to achieve, to do something different, change location, etc. I was in my early twenties and felt that the education system had let me down. I had complied, I had achieved, but I was not fulfilled. I felt like I needed to break out of the cage that society and opportunity, or lack of it, had created for me. I used to focus and think about what I could do with my life, but at that moment, it seemed as if there were no opportunities and wages were low. I started to pray for change, to pray for an opportunity that could create for me a different life and a happier, more rewarding lifestyle.

It was wintertime, and one of my mother's friends invited us to join a group of people for an evening meal at a new Indian restaurant that had just opened in Birmingham. People were raving about it and that we should all go and give it a try. We collected my mother's friend and drove happily to the restaurant. The food was wonderful, full of flavour, and the restaurant was packed with people. There was a general conversation around the table about opportunities, whatever anyone knew of new work in the city, pay, and conditions of service we were sharing. We had a wonderful evening. We drove mom's friend home but then, as we parked the car, we started talking. It was a very dark wet, cold night, and it was now around 10.30 pm. Apart from the sound of rain and wind, everything was still and quiet. There was an air of spookiness as we sat talking in the car.

Mom's friend began telling us of her plight, how short of money they were at the moment and that she had been going to church and praying for a job opportunity that brought in more money. She confessed that sometimes there was not enough money for food in the evening, and she would often be on her knees in the kitchen praying for the next meal. It all seemed so sad, but it also reflected the sentiment of most of us at the dining table earlier. As I was aware of the eeriness of the environment, mom's friend was telling us that one evening she had just arrived home from church, and as she walked up the steep steps to her house, she commented how eerie it felt and that she felt very frightened. She told me how she ran into the house and straight up to the bedroom. Her husband was not due to return home until much later that evening. During the night, she had a nightmare and, upon waking, was aware that she would never feel afraid ever again in her life.

Was this the eeriness I could sense as I was sitting in the car right at this moment? There was certainly interesting energy as I, too, felt almost scared. Just then, a beautiful black cat jumped up on the bonnet of the car, walked up to the windscreen, and looked directly at me. I was so shocked that I screamed, which caused my mom to screen, also. But it was only a black cat. I noticed how the cat looked directly at me, almost trying to read my expression and look deep into my eyes. Very soon, the cat jumped down, and a different feeling came over me.

I knew from that moment onwards my life was about to change! The black cat was an omen for change on a life journey that would take me to the other side of the world and experience the supernatural phenomena of the power of the universal energy, of the spiritual realms, and much much more - to discover in part the true nature of our life and our tremendous abilities which have been suppressed for decades if not centuries by the fear of those who did not possess abilities and had closed minds and hearts.

I felt at that point that my prayers had been heard and answered. Indeed my life changed dramatically several months later. I met my husband, travelled to the other side of the world, changed my career, and experienced different people's lives and cultures.

There are many omens and signs we can all look for. We just need to recognise, feel and be aware of what is happening around us energetically and spiritually. We can do this in part by listening to our inner selves. There is so much noise and distraction around us that we cannot hear or sense what is going on. Often a walk in the park or through the woods will energise us and make us feel better and more relaxed and clears the mind.

I remember well the lucky black cat as my omen for change. Our lives can change at any time and in any direction. Nothing stays the same for a long.

Be aware of your lucky omen. Be it a friendly animal, a signpost, a feather, or maybe a change in the frequency of the environment. Certain tribes have the ability to listen through the wind. Be aware and grateful for divine intervention in your life.

James and Holy Spirit Water

It was bleak living up in the northern part of England. We were living on an RAF base in Lincoln. The area was very open, which aided a frosty, sharp wind. I hadn't long given birth to my beautiful son James, and on an occasional afternoon, a friend with her new baby would join me in a cup of tea and a chat whilst we fed our babies.

I had mentioned to my friend that when I was holding my baby son, I often noticed I became wet with water, and it was not from the baby. I thought not much of it but always thought it rather odd.

One bleak afternoon my friend arrived as planned. I put the kettle on, and we got ourselves warm and comfortable in the lounge. It was a wet, gloomy day and could easily be depressing for someone alone. Very soon, whilst feeding our newborns, we became deep in conversation when all of a sudden, I noticed I was sopping wet as if someone had thrown a glass of water over me. This time I was soaked. My face, arms, and neck were dripping with water. I immediately alerted my friend, who got up out of the comfortable armchair to see what was going on. My friend asked where all the water had come from and immediately looked at the ceiling. The ceiling was dry, no burst pipes. Interestingly I did not feel any water being thrown at me, it just appeared over me. Strangely, this would not be the first or last time this would happen,

We had not long arrived in Sydney, Australia. My husband worked overseas. I had organised the furniture so that the children slept in the same large room. Sometimes when one of the children woke up, I would get into bed with them and cuddle them to sleep. One night I decided to cuddle my son James. Sometime during the night, it felt as if I was woken up. I looked around the room, and all the children were sleeping, so I decided to take the opportunity to visit the bathroom. When I returned, I noticed that my son's forehead and pillow, and the sheets around his neck were wet with water. Something had woken me up prior to the event. There must have been a change in the environment to which I was alerted. Maybe it was a defence mechanism or a survival instinct that took over. To this day, I do not know the reason for the water connection between my son and me. But there was definitely a phenomenon that was taking place from the very early days of his birth.

Needless to say, I get on very well with my son. He is able to sense all my feelings very quickly and sometimes my thoughts. He has always been correct. I have spoken to my son about mediumship and other phenomena, but it does not interest him.

Maybe you have had similar experiences. Are we creating the phenomena, or are we using the universal energy, or is there another phenomenon that we need to research?

The Case of the $50 note

My four young children had gotten together and formed a conspiracy that they wanted to go to the local shop and buy ice cream. As they seemed to be adamant as a unit of four, I felt I had no choice but to say yes. They rarely had sweets or chocolate or biscuits and cake, for that matter. I was always aware of how much sugar they were eating, certainly because of their teeth. This time I gave way. When I looked in my purse, I noticed I didn't have any change; all I had was a $50 note. I was very hesitant, but after much deliberation decided to give them the $50 note. I spoke to them very carefully about holding the money tight and bringing back the change. This was my last $50 for food that week. Off the children set, happy to be able to buy ice cream and feeling important that they held the money. It was not too long before they came back home, stating that they had lost the $50 note and that it had blown away. Well, I could hardly believe it! All our food money is gone in the wind. I could only blame myself for giving the children the note in the first place.

A year to the day, the children went to the local shops. On route, they told me that a $50 note was blown onto the pathway in front of them. They picked it up and ran home, stating we had gotten our $50 note back from last year. I checked with the children if there was anyone around that could have dropped it. But apparently, there was nobody around. We were in the countryside, and there were not many people in the area.

Perhaps the $50 note was apported back to the children exactly one year later? If so, there surely must have been some intelligence that organised it.

Ingram Content Group UK Ltd.
Milton Keynes UK
UKHW022214170423
420327UK00009B/24